GULLIVER'S TRAVELS

Gulliver begins his first journey in 1699 and, after a storm at sea, he finds himself in a country called Lilliput, where the people are only fifteen centimetres tall. He finally escapes and goes home, but soon leaves on another journey – to Brobdingnag, then to Laputa and Luggnagg, and last, to the even stranger country of the Houyhnhnms . . .

As a young man, Gulliver is proud of being human, and proud of his own country, England. When he travels through these strange lands, talking to giants, and magicians, and horses, at first he laughs at their extraordinary ideas and strange opinions. But as the years pass, he begins to wonder and to ask himself questions . . . 'Why do we human beings fight wars, lie, cheat, steal, and kill each other? Isn't there a better way to live?'

OXFORD BOOKWORMS LIBRARY

Classics

Gulliver's Travels

Stage 4 (1400 headwords)

Series Editor: Jennifer Bassett
Founder Editor: Tricia Hedge
Activities Editors: Jennifer Bassett and Alison Baxter

JONATHAN SWIFT

Gulliver's Travels

Retold by
Clare West

Illustrated by
Nick Harris

OXFORD UNIVERSITY PRESS

OXFORD
UNIVERSITY PRESS

Great Clarendon Street, Oxford OX2 6DP

Oxford University Press is a department of the University of Oxford
It furthers the University's objective of excellence in research, scholarship,
and education by publishing worldwide in

Oxford New York

Auckland Bangkok Buenos Aires Cape Town Chennai
Dar es Salaam Delhi Hong Kong Istanbul Karachi Kolkata
Kuala Lumpur Madrid Melbourne Mexico City Mumbai Nairobi
São Paulo Shanghai Saipei Tokyo Toronto

Oxford and Oxford English are registered trade marks of
Oxford University Press in the UK and in certain other countries

ISBN 0 19 423034 1

This simplified edition © Oxford University Press 2000

Fifth impression 2003

First published in Oxford Bookworms 1993
This second edition published in the Oxford Bookworms Library 2000

A complete recording of this Bookworms edition of *Gulliver's Travels*
is available on cassette ISBN 0 19 422781 2

Maps by Martin Ursell

Typeset by Wyvern Typesetting Limited
Printed in Spain by Unigraf s.l.

CONTENTS

1

A voyage to Lilliput

I was born in Nottinghamshire and was the third of five sons. My father was not a rich man, but he was able to send me to Cambridge University, where I studied for three years. When I left college, I continued my studies and became a doctor. But I always wanted to travel, and so I made several voyages as a ship's doctor. When I married my wife Mary, however, I planned to stay at home for a while. But after a few years I discovered I was not earning enough money from my patients. I decided to go to sea again, and this time I joined a ship sailing to the islands in the South Pacific Ocean. We started our journey from Bristol on May 4th, 1699.

At first our voyage went well. We sailed across the Atlantic, round the coast of Africa and into the Indian

Ocean. But before we could reach the Pacific, a violent storm hit us and drove us to the north-west of Tasmania. The wind drove our ship on to a rock, which broke the ship in half. Some of the sailors and I managed to get a boat into the water, and we rowed away to look for land. But when we were too tired to row any more, a great wave hit our small boat, and we all fell into the sea. I do not know what happened to my companions, but I suppose they were all drowned.

The wind and waves pushed me along as I struggled to keep my head above water. I became very tired and soon felt I could not swim any more. Luckily, just then my feet touched the ground. I walked out of the sea and on to a beach, where there was no sign of any people or houses. I was so exhausted that I lay down and went to sleep.

When I woke up next morning, and tried to get up, I could not move. I was lying on my back and my whole body, my arms and legs were strongly fastened to the ground. Even my hair, which was long and thick, was tied to the ground. The sun began to grow hot, and I was very uncomfortable. Soon I felt something alive moving along my leg and up my body to my face, and when I looked down, I saw a very small human being, only fifteen centimetres tall. He had a bow and arrow in his hands, and there were forty more of these little men following him. I was so surprised that I gave a great shout. They all jumped back, very frightened, and some hurt themselves by falling off my body. Meanwhile, I was struggling to unfasten myself, but just as I managed to pull my left arm free of the ropes, I felt a hundred arrows land on my free hand, and more arrows on my face and body. This was very painful, and made me cry aloud. I lay quietly, to see what would happen next.

When they saw I was no longer struggling, they quickly built a platform next to my head, and an official climbed up there to speak to me. Although I could not understand his language, I understood that they would be friendly towards me – if I did not try to harm them. By now I was extremely hungry, so I used sign language to beg the official for food. He seemed to understand me, because immediately ladders were put against my sides and little men climbed up with baskets of food and drink. They were surprised at how much I could eat and drink. In just one mouthful I ate three of their meat dishes and three of their loaves of bread. I drank two of their barrels of wine, and was still thirsty, because that was only half a litre. While they were bringing me food, I wondered whether to pick up a handful of the little men and throw them to their death. But I was afraid they would shoot at me again, and anyway I was grateful for their kindness in giving me food and drink, so I did not move.

After some time, another official climbed up to the platform and spoke to me. From his signs I understood that they were going to move me. The King of this country (which was called Lilliput) had ordered his people to carry me to the capital city, about a kilometre away. I made signs to ask whether I could be untied, but the official politely refused.

While I was eating, a platform had been prepared to carry me. The people of Lilliput, known as the Lilliputians, are very intelligent and clever with their hands. For me, five hundred men built a special wooden platform with twenty-two wheels. Nine hundred of the strongest men worked for about three hours to lift me on to the platform, and one thousand five hundred of the King's largest horses (each eleven and a half centimetres high) pulled me to the capital. I did not know about any of this, because they had put a sleeping powder in my wine, and I was in a deep sleep.

The King had decided I would stay in the largest available

Little men climbed up with baskets of food and drink.

building, just outside the city gates. Its door was only a metre high and half a metre wide, so I could only just get inside on my hands and knees. My guards put ninety-one chains on my left leg, so that I could not escape. Then they cut the ropes that tied me and I was able to get to my feet. As I stood up, I heard cries of astonishment all around me. I felt rather miserable, but at least I could walk about now, in a two-metre circle. I was certainly an interesting sight for the Lilliputians, who had come out of the city in crowds of several thousand to see me.

My guards put chains on my left leg.

Now I had a good view of the countryside. The fields looked like flowerbeds in a garden, and even the tallest trees were only two metres high.

I was soon visited by the King himself. He has a strong, handsome face, and is very popular among his people. He arrived with his Queen, his children, and his lords and ladies, all dressed in beautiful gold and silver clothes. In order to make conversation easier, I lay on my side so that my face was close to him. I spoke to him in all the languages

I knew, but we still could not understand each other.

The King ordered his people to make me a bed, using six hundred Lilliputian beds. It was not very comfortable, but it was better than sleeping on the stone floor. He ordered the crowds of sightseers to go back to their homes, so that the work of the country could continue and I would not be annoyed. For a long time he discussed with his lords in private what should be done with me. I was told all this later by a good friend of mine. Clearly, such a large person could be a danger to his small people. At last it was decided that, as I had behaved so well up to now, I would be kept alive. Food and drink would be brought to me every day from all the villages, six hundred people would be my servants, three hundred men would make me a new suit, and six teachers would teach me their language.

And so in about three weeks I began to speak the language of Lilliput. The King often visited me, and every time he came, I asked him to take off my chains. He explained that first I must promise not to fight against Lilliput or hurt Lilliputians, and that I must be searched for weapons. I agreed to both these things and carefully picked up two of his officers in my hands. I put them first in one pocket, then moved them to all my other pockets, except two which I kept secret. As they searched, they wrote down in a notebook details of all the things they found.

Afterwards I read some of their report:

'In the second coat pocket we found two very large pieces of wood, and inside them were great pieces of metal, very sharp. In another pocket there was a most wonderful engine, at the end of a long chain. The engine was inside a huge round container, which was made half of silver and half of another metal. This second metal was very strange as we could see through it to some mysterious writing and pictures. The engine made a continuous loud noise.'

The officers could not guess what these things were, but they were, of course, my two pocket knives and my watch. They also found my comb, a purse with several gold and silver coins, my gun and bullets.

The King wanted to know what the gun was used for.

'Bring it out,' he ordered me, 'and show me how it works.'

I took the gun out and put a bullet into it.

'Don't be afraid,' I warned the King. Then I fired the gun into the air.

It was the loudest noise the Lilliputians had ever heard. Hundreds of them thought they were dead, and fell down. The King himself was very frightened. As I gave my gun to the officials to keep, I warned them to be careful with it. They allowed me to keep all my other things, and I hoped that one day soon I would be free.

2

Life in Lilliput

I was careful to behave as well as possible, to persuade the King to give me my freedom. Lilliputians soon began to lose their fear of me. They called me the Man-Mountain. Sometimes I lay down and let them dance on my hand, and from time to time children came to play games in my hair. By now I was able to speak their language well.

One day the King invited me to watch the regular entertainments, which are greatly enjoyed by him, his family, and his lords and ladies. I was most interested in the rope-dancing. A very thin rope is fixed thirty centimetres above the ground. People who want to become the King's most important officials jump and dance on this rope, and whoever jumps highest without falling gets the best job. Sometimes the King orders his lords to dance on the rope, to show that they can still do it. This sport is, of course, rather dangerous, and there are occasional deaths as a result. It seems a strange way of choosing officials.

There was another interesting entertainment. The King holds a stick in front of him, and sometimes moves it up and down. One by one, people come up to him and jump over the stick or crawl under it. They go on jumping and crawling as the King moves the stick. The winner is the one who jumps and crawls for the longest time, and he receives a blue ribbon to wear round his waist. The second best

It seems a strange way of choosing officials.

receives a red ribbon, and the third best gets a green one. Many of the Lilliput lords wear their ribbons proudly at all times. I had certainly never seen entertainment like this in any of the countries I had visited before.

Some days later a strange black thing was seen on the beach where I had first arrived in Lilliput. When the people realized it was not alive, they decided that it must belong to the Man-Mountain, and the King ordered them to bring it to me. I thought I knew what it was. When it arrived, it was rather dirty because it had been pulled along the ground by horses. But I was delighted to see that it was in fact my hat. I had lost it in the sea when swimming away from the ship.

I begged the King so often for my freedom that at last he and his lords agreed that I need not be a prisoner any longer. However, I had to promise certain things:
- to help the Lilliputians in war and peace
- to give two hours' warning before a visit to their capital, so that people could stay indoors
- to be careful not to step on any Lilliputians or their animals
- to carry important messages for the King if necessary
- to help the King's workmen carry heavy stones
- to stay in Lilliput until the King allowed me to leave.

On his side the King promised I would receive food and drink, enough for 1,724 Lilliputians. I agreed to everything at once. My chains were broken, and I was free at last!

The first thing I did was visit the capital city. The people were warned, so that they would not be in danger. I stepped carefully over the city wall, which was less than a metre high, and walked slowly through the two main streets. It is usually a very busy city, with shops and markets full of people, but today the streets were empty. There were crowds watching me from every window. In the middle of the city is the King's palace. The King had invited me to enter it, so I stepped over the surrounding wall into the

11

palace garden. But unfortunately the palace itself has walls a metre and a half high around it. I did not want to damage these walls by trying to climb over them. So I walked carefully back out of the city and into the King's park. Here I cut down several of the largest trees with my knife, and made two wooden boxes. When I returned to the palace with my boxes, I was able to stand on one box on one side of the wall and step on to the other box on the other side. I lay down on the ground and looked through the windows, right into the King's rooms. You cannot imagine a more beautiful place to live in. The rooms and furniture are perfect in every detail. As I was looking in, I could see the Queen, surrounded by her lords and ladies. She kindly put her hand out of the window for me to kiss.

The Queen put her hand out of the window for me to kiss.

12

I think I should give you some general information about Lilliput. Most Lilliputians are about fifteen centimetres tall. The birds and animals are, of course, much smaller than the people, and the tallest trees are only a little taller than I am.

All crimes here are punished. But if someone is accused of a crime and then it is proved that the accuser is lying, the accuser is immediately killed. Lilliputians believe that there are two sides to the law. Criminals must be punished, but people of good character must be rewarded. So if a man can prove that he has obeyed every law for six years, he receives a present of money from the King. They also believe that any man who is honest, truthful, and good can serve his King and country. It is more important to have a good character than to be clever or intelligent. However, only those who believe in God are allowed to be the King's officials.

Many of their laws and customs are very different from ours, but human nature is the same in every country. The Lilliputians, like us, have learnt bad ways – choosing officials because they are able to dance on a rope is just one example.

Now I shall return to my adventures in Lilliput. About two weeks after my first visit to the capital, I was visited by one of the King's most important officials. His name was Reldresal, and he had helped me many times since I had arrived in Lilliput.

I started the conversation. 'I'm so glad they've taken away my chains,' I told him.

'Well, my friend,' he answered, 'let me tell you something. You're only free because the King knows we're in a very dangerous situation.'

'Dangerous?' I cried. 'What do you mean?'

'Lilliput has enemies at home and abroad,' he explained. 'For six years now we've had two political groups, the High-Heels and the Low-Heels. Perhaps the High-Heels were more popular in the past, but as you can see, our present King and all his officials wear the lowest heels. The two groups hate each other, and a High-Heel will refuse to

A High-Heel will refuse to speak to a Low-Heel.

speak to a Low-Heel. That's the problem in Lilliput. Now, we're getting information that the people of Blefuscu are going to attack us. Have you heard of Blefuscu? It's an island very near us, almost as large and important as Lilliput. They've been at war with us for three years, you see.'

'But how did this war start?' I asked.

'Well, you know, of course, that most people used to break their boiled eggs at the larger end. But our King's grandfather once cut a finger while breaking his egg this way, and so *his* father the King ordered all Lilliputians, from then on, to break the *smaller* end of their eggs. People who do that are called Small-Endians. But Lilliputians feel strongly about this and some Big-Endians have fought angrily against this law. As many as eleven thousand people have been killed because they refused to break their eggs at the smaller end. Some of the Big-Endians have escaped to join our enemies in Blefuscu. The King of Blefuscu has always wanted to defeat Lilliput in war, and now we hear that he's

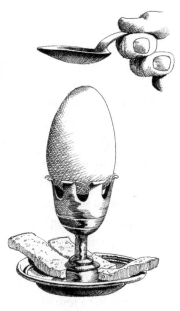

The King ordered everyone to break the smaller end of their eggs.

prepared a large number of ships, which will attack us very soon. So you see, my friend, how much our King needs your help, in order to defeat his enemies.'

I did not hesitate for a moment. 'Please tell the King,' I answered warmly, 'that I am ready to give my life to save him or his country.'

3

Lilliput at war

The island of Blefuscu is only about a kilometre to the north of Lilliput. I knew that just beyond the narrow sea separating the two countries there were at least fifty warships ready to attack us, with many other smaller ships. But I kept away from that side of the coast, so that the people of Blefuscu would not see me. I had a secret plan.

From the King's workmen I ordered fifty heavy metal hooks, each fastened to a piece of strong rope. I took off my coat and shoes, and walked into the sea with the hooks and ropes in my hands. The water was deep in the middle, so I had to swim for a few metres. But it only took me half an hour to get to Blefuscu.

When the Blefuscans saw me, they were so frightened that they jumped out of their ships and swam to the beach. I then used one hook for each ship, and tied all the ropes together at one end. While I was doing this, the enemy shot thousands of arrows at me, which caused me a lot of pain. I was afraid of getting an arrow in my eyes, but I suddenly remembered I still had an old pair of reading glasses in my pocket, so I put them on and continued my work. When I was ready, I started walking into the shallow water away from Blefuscu. As I walked through the waves, I pulled the enemy's warships behind me. When the people of Blefuscu realized that all their warships were disappearing, their cries were terrible to hear.

*As I walked through the waves, I pulled the enemy's
warships behind me.*

As I came nearer to Lilliput, I saw the King and all his
lords and ladies standing on the beach. They could only see
Blefuscu's warships coming closer, as I was swimming and
my head was occasionally under the water. Therefore, they
supposed that I had drowned, and that the Blefuscan ships
were attacking. But when they saw me walking out of the
sea, they welcomed me warmly with cries of astonishment
and delight. The King himself came down to the water to
meet me.

'Everyone in Lilliput is grateful to you!' he cried. 'For your bravery, you will be one of my lords from now on.'

'Thank you, sir,' I replied.

'And now,' he continued, 'go back and steal *all* the enemy's ships, so that we can defeat Blefuscu for ever! We'll destroy the Big-Endians, and I'll become King of the whole world!'

But I would not agree to this plan.

'Sir,' I replied, 'I will never help to take a brave nation's freedom away. Lilliput and Blefuscu should live in peace now.'

The King could not persuade me, and unfortunately he never forgot that I had refused to do what he wanted. Although I had saved his country from attack by Blefuscan warships, he preferred to remember my refusal.

From this time on, I heard from my friends that there were secret conversations in the palace between the King and some of his lords, who were jealous of me. These conversations nearly led to my death in the end.

About three weeks later, the King of Blefuscu sent his officials to ask for peace between the two countries. After the Blefuscans had arranged everything with the Lilliputian officials, they came to visit me. They had heard how I had prevented the King from destroying all their ships. After thanking me, they invited me to visit their country.

However, when I asked the King of Lilliput if I could visit Blefuscu, he agreed, but very coldly. I learnt later that he and some of his lords considered I was wrong to have a conversation with enemies of Lilliput. Now I was beginning to understand how difficult and dangerous political life can be.

A few days later I had another chance to help the King. I was woken at midnight by the cries of hundreds of Lilliputians outside my house.

'Fire! Fire!' they shouted. 'The Queen's rooms in the palace are burning! Come quickly, Man-Mountain!'

So I pulled on my clothes and hurried to the palace. A large part of the building was in flames. People were climbing ladders up the walls, and throwing water on the flames, but the fire was burning more strongly every minute. At least the Queen and her ladies had escaped, but there seemed to be no way of saving this beautiful palace. Suddenly I had an idea. The evening before, I had drunk a lot of good wine, and very luckily I had not made water since then. In three minutes I managed to put out the whole fire, and the lovely old building was safe.

I went home without waiting for the King's thanks, because I was not sure what he would say. Although I had certainly saved the palace, I knew it was a crime, punishable by death, to make water anywhere near the palace. I heard later that the Queen was so angry that she refused to enter any of the damaged rooms ever again, and promised to take her revenge on me.

4

Gulliver escapes from Lilliput

I soon discovered that Flimnap, one of the King's highest officials, was my secret enemy. He had always disliked me, although he pretended to like me, but now he began to suspect his wife of visiting me privately, and he became jealous. Of course his wife did visit me, but always with her daughters and other ladies who came for regular afternoon visits. When visitors arrived at my house, I used to bring the coaches and horses inside, and put them carefully on my table. There was a high edge round the table, so that nobody would fall off. I sat in my chair with my face close

The coaches used to drive around the table.

to the table, and while I was talking to one group of visitors, the others used to drive round the table. I spent many hours like this, in very enjoyable conversation.

In the end Flimnap realized that his wife was not in love with me, and had not done anything wrong, but he was still angry with me. There were other lords who also disliked me, and together they managed to persuade the King that I was a danger to Lilliput. I knew they were discussing me in private, but I was seriously alarmed when I discovered what they had decided. Luckily, as well as Reldresal, I had another good friend among the King's officials. Late one night he visited me secretly, in order to warn me.

'You know,' he began, 'that you've had enemies here for some time. Many of the lords are jealous of your great success against Blefuscu, and Flimnap still hates you. They accuse you of crimes against Lilliput, crimes punishable by death!'

'But . . .' I cried, 'that's not right! I only want to help Lilliput!'

'Listen,' he said. 'I must tell you what I've heard, although my life is in danger if I do. They've accused you of making water in the King's palace, refusing to take all the enemy's ships, refusing to destroy all the Big-Endians, seeing the enemy's officials privately, and planning to visit Blefuscu in order to help the enemy against Lilliput.'

'This is unbelievable!' I cried.

'I must say,' continued my friend, 'that our King reminded his lords how much you had helped the country. But your enemies wanted to destroy you, and they suggested setting fire to your house at night. Then you would die in the fire!'

'What!' I shouted angrily.

'Be quiet, nobody must hear us. Anyway, the King decided *not* to kill you, and that's when your friend Reldresal started speaking. He agreed you'd made mistakes, but said that a good King should always be generous, as our King is. And he suggested that a suitable punishment would be for you to lose your sight. You'd still be strong enough to work for us, but you wouldn't be able to help the Big-Endians.'

I covered my eyes with my hands. I had wanted to help these people and their King. How could they decide to punish me as cruelly as this?

'Your enemies were most disappointed with Reldresal's plan,' my friend went on. 'They said you were a Big-Endian in your heart, and reminded the King how much you cost Lilliput in food and drink. Reldresal spoke again, to suggest saving money by giving you a little less food every day. In this way you'd become ill, and in a few months you'd die. And so they all agreed. In three days Reldresal will be sent to explain your punishment to you. He'll inform you that the King has been very kind to you, and that you're lucky to lose only your eyes. You'll be tied down, and very sharp arrows will be shot into your eyes. The King's doctors will make sure that you can no longer see.'

'This is terrible news!' I said, 'but thank you for warning me, my dear friend.'

'You alone must decide what to do,' he replied, 'and now I must leave you, so that nobody suspects me of warning you.'

When I was alone, I thought about the situation for a long time. Perhaps I was wrong, but I could not see that the King was being kind and generous in ordering such an inhuman punishment. What should I do? I could ask for a trial, but I was not confident of the judges' honesty. I could attack the capital and kill all the Lilliputians, but when I remembered the King's past kindness to me, I did not want to do that.

At last I decided to escape. And so, before Reldresal came to tell me of my punishment, I went to the north of Lilliput, where our ships lay. I took my clothes off and put them into one of the largest warships. I also put a blanket into it. Then I stepped into the sea, and swam to Blefuscu. By pulling the Lilliput warship behind me, I kept my clothes and blanket dry.

When I arrived, the King of Blefuscu sent two guides to show me the way to the capital. There I met the King, the Queen and the lords and ladies in their coaches. I explained that I had come to visit Blefuscu, as I had been invited. However, I did not say anything about the punishment waiting for me in Lilliput. They welcomed me warmly. That night, as there was no building big enough for me, I slept on the ground, covered by my blanket. It was not as comfortable as my bed in Lilliput, but I did not mind.

I did not spend long in Blefuscu. Only three days after my

arrival, I noticed a boat in the sea, near the beach. It was a real boat, large enough for me. Perhaps it had been driven there by a storm. I swam out to it and tied ropes to it. Then, with the help of twenty of Blefuscu's ships and three thousand sailors, I pulled it on to the beach. It was not badly damaged, and it was exciting to be able to start planning my journey back to England and my home.

During this time, the King of Lilliput had written to ask the King of Blefuscu to send me back, as a prisoner, so that I could receive my punishment. The King of Blefuscu, however, replied that I was too strong to be taken prisoner, and that I would soon be returning to my country anyway. Secretly he invited me to stay and help him in Blefuscu, but I no longer believed in the promises of kings or their officials, so I politely refused.

I was now impatient to start my voyage home, and the King ordered his workmen to repair the boat and prepare everything I needed. I had the meat of one hundred cattle and three hundred sheep to eat on the journey, and I also had some live animals to show to my friends in England.

About one month later, I left Blefuscu, on September 24th, 1701. The King, the Queen

I had some live animals to show to my friends.

and their lords and ladies all came down to the beach to wave goodbye.

After sailing all day, I reached a small island, where I slept that night. On the third day, September 26th, I saw a sail, and was delighted to discover that it was an English ship, on its way home to England. The captain picked me up, and I told him my story. At first he thought I was mad, but when I took the live animals out of my pocket to show him, he believed me.

We arrived home at last on April 13th, 1702, and I saw my dear wife and children again. At first I was delighted to be at home again. I earned quite a lot of money by showing my Lilliputian animals to people, and in the end I sold them for a high price. But as the days passed, I became restless, and wanted to see more of the world. And so, only two months later, I said goodbye to my family and sailed away again.

5

A voyage to Brobdingnag

I left Bristol on June 20th, 1702, in a ship which was sailing to India. We had good sailing weather until we reached the Cape of Good Hope in South Africa, where we landed to get fresh water. We had to stay there for the winter, however, because the ship needed repairs and the captain was ill. In the spring we left Africa and sailed round the island of Madagascar into the Indian Ocean. But on 19th April the wind began to blow very violently from the west, and we were driven to the east of the Molucca Islands. On 2nd May the wind stopped blowing and the sea was calm. But our captain, who knew that part of the world very well, warned us that there would be a storm the next day. So we prepared the ship as well as we could, and waited.

The captain was right. On 3rd May the wind began to get stronger. It was a wild, dangerous wind, blowing from the south this time. We had to take down our sails as the storm hit our ship. Huge waves crashed down on to us, and the wind drove our helpless ship eastwards into the Pacific Ocean.

For several days we struggled with the wind and waves, but at last the storm died away and the sea was calm again. Luckily, our ship was not badly damaged, but we had been driven over two thousand kilometres to the east. None of us knew exactly where we were, so the captain decided to continue sailing eastwards, where we had never been before. We sailed on for another two weeks.

Finally, on 16th June, 1703, we saw a large island with a small piece of land joined to it. I later discovered that this country was called Brobdingnag. The captain sent some of his sailors in a boat to land there and bring back some fresh water. I went with them because I was interested in seeing a new country. We were delighted to be on land again, and while the men looked for a river or a lake, I walked for about a kilometre away from the beach.

When I returned, to my astonishment I saw that the

sailors were already in the boat. They were rowing as fast
as they could towards the ship! I was going to shout to tell
them they had forgotten me, when suddenly I saw a huge
creature walking after them into the sea. I realized he could
not catch them, because they had nearly got to the ship, but
I did not wait to see the end of that adventure. I ran away
from him as fast as possible, and did not stop until I found
myself in some fields. The grass was about seven metres
high, and the corn about thirteen metres high. It took me an
hour to cross just one field, which had a hedge at least forty
metres high. The trees were much taller than that. Just as I
was trying to find a hole in the hedge, so that I could get into

I was trying to find a hole in the hedge.

the next field, I saw another giant coming towards me. He seemed as tall as a mountain, and every one of his steps measured about ten metres.

In fear and astonishment I hid in the corn, and hoped he would not notice me. He shouted in a voice like thunder, and seven other giants appeared. They seemed to be his servants. When he gave the order, they began to cut the corn in the field where I was hiding. As they moved towards me, I moved away, but at last I came to a part of the field where rain had knocked down the corn. There was no longer anywhere for me to hide, and I knew I would be cut to pieces by the giants' sharp knives. I lay down and prepared to die. I could not stop myself thinking of Lilliput. There, I myself had been a giant, an important person who had become famous for helping the people of that small country. Here, it was the opposite. I was like a Lilliputian in Europe, and I began to understand how a very small creature feels.

Suddenly I noticed that one of the giants was very close to me. As his huge foot rose over my head, I screamed as loudly as I could. He looked around on the ground, and finally saw me. He stared at me for a moment, then very carefully, he picked me up with finger and thumb and looked at me. I was now twenty metres up in the air, and I desperately hoped he would not decide to throw me to the ground. I did not struggle, and spoke politely to him, although I knew he did not understand any of my languages. He took me to the farmer, who soon realized that I was not an animal, but an intelligent being. He carefully put me in his pocket and took me home to show to his wife. When she saw me, she screamed and jumped back in fear, perhaps thinking I was an insect. But in a little while she became used to me, and was very kind to me.

6

Gulliver and his master

Soon after we arrived, the whole family sat down at the table for dinner. There was a large piece of meat on a plate about eight metres across. The farmer put me on the table, with some small pieces of bread and meat in front of me. I was very frightened of falling off the edge of the table, which was ten metres from the ground. The farmer and his family were delighted to watch me eating food with my own small knife and fork. But when I started walking across the table to the farmer, his youngest son, a boy of about ten, picked me up by the legs. He held me so high in the air that my whole body trembled. Fortunately his father took me away at once, and angrily hit the boy hard on the head. But I remembered how cruel children can be to small animals, and I did not want the boy to take his revenge on me. So I fell on my knees and asked them not to punish the child any more. They seemed to understand.

Just then I heard a noise behind me. It sounded like twelve machines running at the same time. I turned my head and saw a huge cat, three times larger than one of our cows. The farmer's wife held it in her arms, so that it could not jump at me. But in fact, because I showed no fear, there was no danger, and the cat even seemed a little afraid of me.

At the end of dinner, a servant came in with the farmer's one-year-old son in her arms. He immediately started crying and screaming, because he wanted to play with me. His mother smiled and put me in his hand. When he picked me up and put my head in his mouth, I shouted so loudly that he dropped me. Luckily, I was not hurt, but it showed me how dangerous life was going to be in Brobdingnag.

After eating, the farmer, or my master, as I shall now call him, went back to his work in the fields. I think he told his wife to take good care of me, because she put me carefully on her bed and locked the bedroom door. I was exhausted, and slept for two hours.

When I woke up, I felt very small and lonely in such a huge room, and on such a large bed. Suddenly I saw two huge rats run towards me across the bed. One came right up to my face, so I pulled out my sword and cut open his stomach. The other ran away at once. I walked up and down on the bed, to control my trembling legs, and looked at the dead rat. It was as large as a big dog, and its tail measured two metres. When my master's wife came into the room some time later, I showed her how I had killed the rat. She was delighted that I was not hurt, and threw the dead rat out of the window.

I saw two huge rats run towards me across the bed.

My master had a daughter who was about nine years old. She was given the special responsibility of taking care of me, and I owe her my life. During my stay in her country we were always together, and she saved me from many dangerous situations. I called her Glumdalclitch, which means 'little nurse'. She was good at sewing, and managed to make some clothes for me in the thinnest material available. She also made me a small bed, which was placed on a shelf too high for rats to reach. Perhaps the most useful thing she did was to teach me the language, so that in a few days I could speak it quite well.

Soon all my master's neighbours were talking about the strange little creature he had found in a field. One of them came to see me, and as I walked towards him across the table, he put on his glasses. His eyes behind the glasses looked like the full moon shining into two windows. I thought this was very funny, and laughed loudly. Unfortunately, that made him very angry. I heard him whispering to my master all evening, and I was sorry I had laughed at him.

Next day Glumdalclitch came to me in tears.

'You'll never guess what's happened!' she told me sadly. 'Our neighbour has advised Father to show you to people, for money! Father's going to take you to market tomorrow, where there'll be crowds of people ready to pay for entertainment! I'm so ashamed! And perhaps you'll get hurt! Other people won't be as careful with you as I am!'

'Don't worry, Glumdalclitch,' I replied. 'As I'm a stranger here, I don't mind being shown to people like a strange wild animal. I must do what your father wants.' I was secretly hoping I would one day find a way of escaping and returning to my own country.

So the next day my master and his daughter got on their huge horse. Glumdalclitch carried me inside a small box, which had air-holes so that I could breathe. When we arrived at the market town, my master hired the largest room in the public house, and placed me upon the table there. His daughter stayed close to me to make sure that nobody hurt me. I was told to speak in their language, pull out my sword, drink from a cup, and do other things to amuse the crowd. Only thirty people were allowed in to see me at one time. On that first day everybody wanted to see me, and I was shown to over three hundred and fifty people.

My master's plan was so successful that he arranged to

show me again on the next market day. I did not look forward to this at all. I was so tired with the journey and the entertainment that I could only walk and speak with difficulty for the next three days. Even when we were at home, neighbours and friends from all parts of the country came to look at me, and my master made me work hard to amuse them. So I had almost no rest.

My master finally realized that he could make a fortune by showing me to people all over the country. So about two months after my arrival in Brobdingnag, we left the farm and started our journey to the capital. As before, Glumdalclitch came with us, to take care of me. On the way we stopped in many towns and villages, so that I could be shown to people. At last, after a journey of nearly five thousand kilometres, we arrived at the capital. Now I had to work even harder, as people came to look at me ten times a day.

7

At the King's palace

Although Glumdalclitch tried to make things as comfortable as possible for me, such an exhausting life was beginning to have a bad effect on my health. I was becoming thinner and thinner. When my master noticed this, he thought I would not live much longer. But it was clear that he wanted to make as much money out of me as he could. While he was thinking how to do this, he was asked to bring me to the palace. The Queen and her ladies had heard about me and wanted to see me. When we arrived in front of the Queen, I fell on my knees and begged to be allowed to kiss her foot. But she kindly held out her hand to me. I took her little finger in both my arms, and put it very politely to my lips.

She seemed very pleased with me, and finally she said, 'Would you enjoy living here in the palace, do you think?'

'Great queen,' I answered, 'I must do what my master wants, but if I were free, I would want to spend my whole life obeying your orders.'

She immediately arranged to buy me from my master. He was delighted to receive a good price for me, especially as he felt sure I would not live longer than a month. I also begged the Queen to let Glumdalclitch stay with me, because she had always taken such good care of me. The Queen agreed, and Glumdalclitch could not hide her happiness.

When my master had left the palace alone, the Queen said to me, 'Why didn't you say goodbye to him? And why did you look at him so coldly?'

'Madam, I must tell you,' I replied, 'that since he found me, my master has used me as an easy way of making money for himself. He's made me work so hard that I feel tired and ill. He's sold me to you only because he thinks I'm going to die soon. But I feel better already, now that I belong to such a great and good queen.'

The Queen was clearly surprised to hear such intelligent words from such a small creature, and decided to show me

The King thought I must be a toy.

to her husband. When the King saw me, he thought at first that I must be a mechanical toy. However, when he heard my answers to his questions, he realized I must be alive, and he could not hide his astonishment.

To discover what kind of animal I was, he sent for three of his cleverest professors. After looking at me carefully, they decided that I was a creature outside the laws of nature. I was much too small to climb their trees, or dig their fields, or kill and eat their animals. They could not understand where I had come from, or how I could possibly survive. And when I told them that in my country there were millions just like me, they did not believe me, but just smiled. However, the King was more intelligent than they were. After speaking to Glumdalclitch and questioning me again, he realized that my story must be true.

They took very good care of me. The Queen's workmen made a special bedroom for me. It was a wooden box, with windows, a door, and two cupboards. The ceiling could be lifted off, so that Glumdalclitch could change my sheets and tidy my room. The workmen even made me two little chairs and a table, and a lock for the door, so that no rats could get in.

The Queen became so fond of me that she could not eat without me. My small table and chair were always placed on the dinner table near her left elbow, and Glumdalclitch stood near me, in case I needed her help. I ate off tiny silver plates, with silver knives and forks. But I never got used to seeing the Queen eat. In one mouthful she ate as much as twelve English farmers could eat in a whole meal. She drank from a cup as big as one of our barrels, and her knives were like huge swords. I was quite frightened of them.

On Wednesday, which is a day of rest in Brobdingnag, like our Sunday, the King and Queen always had dinner together, with their children, in the King's rooms. I was usually invited too. My little chair and table were at the King's left elbow. He enjoyed very much hearing me talk about England – our laws, our universities, our great buildings. He listened so politely that I perhaps talked a little too much about my dear country. In the end he looked at me kindly, but could not stop himself laughing. He turned to one of his lords.

'How amusing it is,' he said to him, 'that an insect like this should talk of such important matters! He thinks his country is so highly developed! But I suppose even tiny creatures like him have a hole in the ground that they call a home. They argue, they love, they fight and they die, as we do. But of course the poor little animals aren't on our level.'

I could not believe what I was hearing. He was laughing at my country, a country famous for its beautiful cities and palaces, its great kings and queens, its brave and honest people. However, there was nothing I could do about it, and I simply had to accept the situation.

The worst problem I had at the palace was the Queen's dwarf. Until I arrived, he had always been the smallest person in the country (he was about ten metres tall). As I was much smaller than him, he was very rude to me and behaved very badly, especially when nobody was looking. Once he took a large bone from the table and stood it on the Queen's plate. Then he took me in both hands and pushed my legs into the top of the bone. I could not pull myself out,

The dwarf pushed my legs into the top of the bone.

37

and had to stay there, feeling – and looking – extremely stupid. When the Queen finally saw me, she could not stop herself laughing, but she was angry with the dwarf at the same time.

In Brobdingnag there are large numbers of flies in summer, and these awful insects, each as big as an English bird, gave me no peace. The dwarf used to catch some in his hands, and then let them out suddenly under my nose. He did this both to frighten me and amuse the Queen. I had to use my knife to cut them to pieces as they flew around me.

Another time, the dwarf picked me up and dropped me quickly into a bowl of milk on the table. Luckily, I am a good swimmer, so I managed to keep my head out of the milk. As soon as Glumdalclitch saw I was in danger, she ran from the other side of the room to rescue me. I was not hurt, but this time the dwarf was sent away from the palace as a punishment. I was very pleased.

I would now like to describe Brobdingnag. The people who draw our European maps think there is nothing but sea between Japan and America, but they are wrong. Brobdingnag is quite a large country, joined on to north-west America, but separated from the rest of America by high mountains. It is about ten thousand kilometres long and from five to eight thousand wide. The sea around it is so rough and there are so many rocks in the water that no large ships can land on any of the beaches. This means that the people of Brobdingnag do not normally have visitors from other parts of the world.

There are fifty-one cities and a large number of towns and villages. The capital stands on both sides of a river, and has more than eighty thousand houses. It covers three hundred and forty square kilometres. The King's palace covers about eleven square kilometres: the main rooms are eighty metres high. The palace kitchen is huge – if I described it, with its great pots on the fire and the mountains of food on the tables, perhaps you would not believe me. Travellers are often accused of not telling the truth when they return. To avoid this happening to me, I am being careful to describe what I saw as exactly and carefully as possible.

8

More adventures in Brobdingnag

Because I was so small, I had several dangerous accidents during my stay at the palace. One day Glumdalclitch put me down on the grass in the palace garden, while she went for a walk with some of the Queen's ladies. A small white dog which belonged to one of the gardeners appeared, and seemed very interested in me. He took me in his mouth and carried me to his master. Luckily, he had been well trained, and did not try to bite me, so I was not hurt.

One day the Queen said to me, 'It would be good for your health to do some rowing or sailing. What do you think? Would you like me to arrange it for you?'

'Madam,' I answered, 'I'd love to row or sail a little every day. But where can we find a boat that's small enough?'

'Leave that to me,' she replied, and called for her workmen. She ordered them to make a tiny boat with sails. They also made a wooden container, about a hundred metres long, seventeen metres wide and three metres deep. This container was filled with water, and I was carefully placed in my boat on the water. Every day I used to row or sail there, while the Queen and her ladies watched. There was no wind, of course, but the ladies blew hard to move my boat along.

I nearly lost my life again, when a lady picked me up to put me in the boat. She was not careful enough, and dropped me. With horror, I felt myself falling through the air. But instead of crashing to the ground, I was caught, by my trousers, on a pin in her clothes. I had to stay there without moving a finger, until Glumdalclitch came running to rescue me.

But the greatest danger to me in Brobdingnag came from a monkey. One day Glumdalclitch left me alone in her bedroom while she visited some of the ladies. It was a warm day, and her window was open. I was in the box which I used as my bedroom, with the door open. Suddenly I heard the noise of an animal jumping through the window, and immediately I hid at the back of my box. The monkey, which appeared huge to me, very soon discovered my hiding-place. He picked me up, and held me close to him like a baby. When he heard someone opening the bedroom door, he jumped out of the window and ran on to the roof.

I thought I had never been in such great danger. He was running on three legs and holding me in the fourth. At any moment he could let me fall, and we were at least three hundred metres above the ground. I could hear a lot of shouting in the palace. The servants had realized what was happening, and brought ladders to climb up on to the roof. Glumdalclitch was crying, and hundreds of people were watching from the garden. Meanwhile, the monkey was sitting calmly on top of the roof. He was taking food from his mouth and trying to push it into *my* mouth. He still seemed to think I was his baby. I suppose it was an amusing

41

sight for the crowd below, but I was in terrible fear of falling.

The monkey still seemed to think I was his baby.

Finally, several servants climbed on the roof, and as they came nearer, the monkey put me down and ran away. I was rescued and brought down to the ground. I had to stay in bed for two weeks after this, before I felt well enough to meet people again. The monkey was caught and killed.

When I next saw the King, he asked me about this experience. 'How did you feel,' he said, 'when the monkey was holding you up on the roof?'

'Sir,' I replied bravely, 'I was afraid, that's true. But next time an animal like that attacks me, I shall not hesitate. I'll pull out my sword like this' – and I showed him what I would do – 'and give the creature such a wound that it will never come near me again!'

But while I waved my tiny sword in the air, the King and his lords laughed loudly. I had wanted to prove my bravery, but I failed, because to them I was only an unimportant little creature. I realized later that this often happens in England, when *we* laugh at someone of no family, fortune, or intelligence, who pretends to be as important as our great leaders.

In the next few weeks, I began to have some very interesting conversations with the King. He was an intelligent, understanding person.

'Tell me more about your country,' he said to me one day. 'I would like to hear about your laws, your political life, and your customs. Tell me everything. There may be something that we can usefully copy here in Brobdingnag.'

'I shall be delighted, sir,' I answered proudly. 'Our king

controls our three great countries, Scotland, Ireland and England. We grow much of our own food, and our weather is neither too hot nor too cold. There are two groups of men who make our laws. One is called the House of Lords – they are men from the oldest and greatest families in the country. The other is called the House of Commons – these are the most honest, intelligent, and sensible men in the country, and are freely chosen by the people. We have judges to decide punishments for criminals, and we have a large army, which cannot be defeated by any other in the world.'

While I was talking, the King was making notes. For several days I continued my explanation, and I also described British history over the last hundred years. Then the King asked me a large number of questions. These were some of them.

'How do you teach and train young people of good family? If the last son of an old family dies, how do you make new lords for the House of Lords? Are these lords really the most suitable people to make the country's laws? And in the House of Commons, are these men really so honest and intelligent? Do rich men never buy their way in to this House? You say the lawmakers receive no pay, but are you sure that they never accept bribes?'

Then he asked questions about our lawcourts. 'Why are your trials so long and so expensive? How much do your lawyers and judges really know about the laws? How carefully do they decide between right and wrong?

'And why,' he went on, 'are you so often at war? Either you enjoy fighting, or you have very difficult neighbours! Why do you need an army at all? You would not be afraid of any other country, if you were peaceful people. And in

While I was talking, the King was making notes.

the last hundred years you've done nothing but rob, fight, and murder! Your recent history shows the very worst effects of cruelty, jealousy, dishonesty, and madness!'

45

I tried to answer the King as well as I could, but he did not think our system was a good one.

'No, my little friend,' he said kindly but seriously, 'I'm sorry for you. You've proved to me that your country has nothing valuable to offer us. Perhaps once, in the past, your political life was adequately organized, but now it is clear that there is laziness and selfishness in every part of the system. Your politicians can be bribed, your soldiers aren't really brave, your judges and lawyers are neither reasonable nor honest, and your lawmakers themselves know little and do less. I sincerely hope that you, who have spent most of your life travelling, have a better character than most Englishmen. But from what you've told me, I'm afraid that your countrymen are the worst little nation of insects that has ever crawled upon the ground.'

I am very sorry to have to report these words of the King's, and I only do so because of my love of the truth. I must tell you exactly what happened, even if I do not agree with it. I had to listen patiently, while he was giving his extraordinary opinions of my dear country. We must remember, however, that this King lives in a country almost completely separate from the rest of the world. Because he does not know other countries' systems or customs, he has a certain narrowness of thinking, which we Europeans do not have, of course.

You will find it difficult to believe what happened next.

'Sir,' I said, 'I'd like to give you something to thank you for your kindness to me since I arrived at the palace. Three or four hundred years ago, we Europeans discovered how to make a special powder. When you set fire to it, it burns and explodes immediately, with a noise louder than thunder. You can use it to shoot heavy balls of metal from large guns. It can destroy the largest ships, it can kill a whole army, it can cut men's bodies in half, it can destroy the strongest walls. It's called gunpowder, and it's easy and cheap to make. To show you how grateful I am to you, I'm offering to explain how to make it – then you will be able to destroy all your enemies!'

I was very surprised by the King's reply.

'No!' he cried in horror. 'Don't tell me! I don't want to know how to murder people like that. I would rather give half my country away than know the secret of this powder. How can a tiny creature like you have such inhuman, cruel ideas? Never speak to me of this again!'

How strange that such an excellent king should not take the chance I was offering him! No European king would hesitate for a moment. But he had other strange ideas. He believed, very simply, that every problem can be solved by honest, sensible people, and that the political life of a country must have no secrets and must be open for all to see and understand. Of course, we know that this is impossible, so perhaps his opinion of us is not worth considering.

9

Gulliver escapes from Brobdingnag

I was still hoping to return to England one day. But the ship in which I had arrived in Brobdingnag was the first that had ever come near the coast. So I could not see how I could get away. I began to think more and more about my family and my home.

By now I had been in Brobdingnag for about two years. When the King and Queen travelled to the south coast, Glumdalclitch and I went with them. I really wanted to be close to the sea again, which I had not seen or even smelt for so long. As Glumdalclitch was ill, I asked a young servant to take me down to the beach for some fresh air. The boy carried me in my travelling box, and put me down on the beach, while he looked for birds' eggs among the rocks. I looked sadly at the sea, but stayed in my box, and after a while I fell asleep.

I was woken suddenly when my box was lifted high in the air. I can only suppose that a large bird took hold of the ring on top of the box with his talons, and flew away with it. Through the windows I could see the sky and clouds passing by, and I could hear the noise of the bird's wings. Then I was falling, so fast that I felt quite breathless. There was a loud crash, as the box fell into the sea. Perhaps the bird had been attacked by others, and so had to drop what he was carrying.

*I can only suppose that a large bird took hold of the ring
on the top of the box with his talons.*

Luckily, the box had been well made, and not much sea water came in. But I do not think any traveller has ever been in a worse situation than I was then. I wondered how long I would survive, with no food or drink in the middle of the ocean. I felt sure I would never see poor Glumdalclitch again, and I knew how sad she would be to lose me.

Several hours passed, and then I suddenly heard a strange noise above my head. People were fastening a rope to the ring. Then my box was pulled through the water. Was it a ship that was pulling me along?

'Help! Help!' I shouted as loudly as I could.

I was delighted to hear English voices reply.

'Who's there?' they cried.

'I'm English!' I shouted back desperately. 'Please help me to get out of here! Just put your finger into the ring on top of the box and lift it out of the water! Quickly!'

There were great shouts of laughter.

'He's mad!' I heard one man say.

'*Ten men* couldn't lift that huge box!' said another. There was more laughter.

Indeed, because I had been with giants for so long, I had forgotten that my countrymen were as small as me. The only thing the sailors could do was to cut a hole in the top of my box, and help me to climb out. I was exhausted and unable to walk far.

They took me to their captain.

'Welcome to my ship,' he said kindly. 'You're lucky we found you. My men saw that huge box on the water, and we decided to pull it along behind the ship. Then we realized there was a man inside! Why were you locked up in there? Was it a punishment for some terrible crime? But tell me all about it later. Now you need to sleep, and then eat.'

When I told him my story, a few hours later, he found it difficult to believe. But after a while he began to accept that what I told him must be true.

'But why do you shout so loudly?' he asked. 'We can hear you perfectly well if you speak normally.'

'You see,' I explained, 'for two years I've had to shout to make myself understood by the giants. I was like a man in the street who was trying to talk to another man at the top of a very tall building. And another thing – your sailors all seem very small to me, because I've been used to looking up at people twenty metres tall.'

He shook his head. 'Well, what a story! I think you should write a book about it when you get home.'

I stayed on the ship for several months, as we sailed slowly home to England. Finally, we arrived in Bristol on June 3rd, 1706. When I reached home, my wife made me promise never to go to sea again, and I thought my adventures had come to an end.

10

The flying island of Laputa

I had only been at home for about ten days when a friend of mine asked me to join him on a journey to the East Indies. I still wanted to see more of the world, and as he was offering to give me double the usual pay, I managed to persuade my wife to let me go. The voyage took eight months, and after stopping for a short time in Malaysia, we arrived in the Gulf of Tongking.

'I'll have to stay here for a while on business,' my friend the captain told me. 'But you can take the ship and some of the sailors. Go and see what you can buy and sell in the islands around here.' That sounded interesting to me, so I agreed.

Unfortunately, we sailed straight into a terrible storm, which drove us many miles eastward. Then, by a very unlucky chance, we were seen and chased by two pirate ships. Our ship was not fast enough to escape, and the pirates caught us. They decided to keep the sailors to help sail the ship, but they did not need me. I suppose I was lucky they did not kill me. Instead, they left me alone in a small boat in the middle of the ocean, with only enough food for a few days, while they sailed away.

I am sure the pirates thought I would die. However, I saw land some hours later, and I managed to sail the boat to it. As I stepped out of the boat and walked up the beach, I

Our ship was not fast enough to escape, and the pirates caught us.

noticed that although the sun had been very hot, the air suddenly seemed cooler. At first I thought a cloud was passing over the sun. But when I looked up, I saw, to my great astonishment, a large island in the sky, between me and the sun. It was moving towards me, and there were people running around on it. I waved my arms and shouted as loudly as possible. 'Help! Help!' I cried. 'Rescue me!'

53

When the island was about a hundred metres over my head, they let down a seat on a chain. I sat on it, and was pulled up to the island. I had discovered the flying island of Laputa.

I sat on the seat, and was pulled up to the island.

Laputans are certainly strange-looking people. Their heads always turn either to right or left: one of their eyes turns inwards, the other upwards. Their main interests are music and mathematics. They spend so much time thinking about mathematical problems that they do not notice what is happening around them. In fact, rich Laputans employ a servant whose job is to follow his master everywhere. The servant warns him if he is going to step into a hole, and reminds him to reply if someone speaks to him.

I was taken to see the King, but had to wait for at least an hour while he struggled with a difficult mathematical question. However, when he had finished, he spoke politely to me, and ordered his servants to show me to a room. For dinner they gave me three kinds of meat – a square of beef, a triangle of chicken and a circle of lamb. Even the bread was cut into mathematical shapes. In the evening a teacher arrived to help me learn the language, and in a few days I was able to make conversation with the island people.

Laputa is a circle of land, about eight kilometres across, covered with houses and other buildings. It is moved by a simple machine which uses magnets to pull the island closer to land or push it higher into the sky. The island always moves slowly. It can only fly over the country called Balnibarbi, which belongs to the King of Laputa.

It is difficult talking to Laputans, as they have little interest in anything except music and mathematics. They are, however, very worried about the future of the earth, the sun, and the stars, and they often discuss this. I heard a conversation about this shortly before I left Laputa.

'How are you, my friend?' one man asked another.

'As well as can be expected,' came the reply.

'And how is the sun, do you think?'

'I thought he looked rather feverish this morning. I'm afraid he'll get too hot and destroy himself one day, if he goes on like this.'

'I know, it's very worrying. And what about the earth? It's only thirty years until the next falling star comes this way, and the earth was very nearly destroyed by the last one!'

'That's right. We know that the next falling star is almost certain to get too close to the sun, and catch fire! And when the earth passes through that fire, it'll be destroyed immediately!'

'Only thirty years! That's not much to look forward to, is it?' And the two men shook their heads sadly.

After several months on the island, I asked if I could visit the country underneath us. The King agreed, and ordered his officials to put me down on Balnibarbi, and show me round the capital, Lagado.

The most interesting place I saw there was the university, which was full of very clever men, with very clever ideas. They were all working hard to find better, faster, cheaper, easier ways of doing and making things. They had ideas for building houses from the roof downwards, turning rocks into soft material, making rivers run uphill, and saving sunshine in bottles. I cannot remember half of the astonishingly clever ideas which they were working on. One day, they told me, they would find the answers to all these problems, and then their country would be the most wonderful place in the world. Meanwhile, I noticed that the people looked hungry and miserable. Their clothes were old and full of holes, their houses were badly built and falling down. There were no vegetables or corn growing in the fields.

When I visited the School of Mathematics, I could not understand why the students looked so unhappy.

'What's the matter, young man?' I asked one of them. 'You look quite ill.'

'Yes, sir,' he answered. 'You see, we've only just eaten our lessons for today, and it's made us feel rather sick.'

'*Eaten* them?' I repeated in surprise. 'Why did you do that?'

'Oh, that's the way we learn here, sir,' he replied. 'Our professors write mathematical questions and answers on paper, then we eat the paper. After that we're only supposed to have bread and water for three days, while the information moves upwards to our heads. But it's awful, sir, not eating much for three days. And we often feel sick. Er . . . excuse me, sir!' And he ran past me out of the room. This highly developed system of teaching did not seem to be working well.

11

Glubbdubdrib and Luggnagg

Although the Laputans were kind to me, I did not want to spend a long time in their country. Therefore, I decided to travel from Balnibarbi to the island of Luggnagg, from there to Japan, and then home to England. But before I went to Luggnagg, an official I had met in Lagado persuaded me to visit the small island of Glubbdubdrib.

'You'll find it a very interesting place,' he told me. 'Glubbdubdrib means the island of magicians. All the important people there are good at magic, you see. The President is the best magician of them all. But I must warn you, he has some very strange servants – they're all ghosts! By using magic he can order the ghost of any dead person to be his servant for twenty-four hours, and the ghost must obey.'

It seemed unbelievable, but it was true. When we arrived on the island, we were invited to the President's palace. His servants certainly looked strange to me – there was a smell of death about them. When the President no longer needed them, he waved a hand, and they simply disappeared.

I visited the President every day during my stay, and soon got used to seeing the ghosts. One day the President said, 'Gulliver, would you like to call a ghost? It could be anyone from the beginning of the world up to the present day. You could ask them questions about their lives. And you can be sure they'll tell the truth – ghosts always do.'

'That's very kind of you, sir,' I replied, and thought hard for a moment. 'First, I'd like to see Alexander the Great, please.'

The President pointed out of the window. There in a large field was the ghost of Alexander, with his huge army. This famous king lived long ago in Macedonia in northern Greece. His kingdom covered many countries, from Greece to Egypt, from Persia to parts of India. But he died very young, when he was only thirty-three, and no one knew why. The President called him into the room.

'Great King,' I said to him, 'just tell me one thing. Were you murdered, or did you die naturally?'

'Young man,' he replied, 'nobody murdered me. I drank too much and died of a fever.'

So, in these few words, I had learnt one of the secrets of history! I turned to the President. 'And now, may we see Julius Caesar and Brutus?'

The two Romans took Alexander's place. Brutus, of course, had killed Julius Caesar in Rome on 15th March, 44BC – one of the most famous murders in history. It is terrible to die by the hand of a friend.

'Great Caesar,' I said, 'how do you feel about your murderer, Brutus?'

'Do not call him that,' replied Caesar. 'He is a brave, good man, the best in Rome, and he did the right thing for Rome by killing me. In death, as in life, he has always been my friend.'

I cannot remember how many more ghosts I called to appear. I was very interested in their answers to my questions, which often seemed to offer a different view of history from the one I had been taught at school.

However, it was soon time to leave Glubbdubdrib, and sail to Luggnagg, a much larger island to the south-east of Japan. The Luggnuggians are polite and generous people, and I stayed here for three months. I made many friends among them. One day, one of them asked me, 'Have you ever seen any of our Struldbrugs?'

'Great Caesar,' I said, 'how do you feel about your
murderer, Brutus?'

'I don't think so,' I replied. 'What's that?'

'Well, a Struldbrug is a human being who will never die, but will live for ever. If a Luggnuggian baby is born with a round spot above its left eye, which never disappears, it's a Struldbrug. We have over a thousand of them in the country.'

'How wonderful!' I cried. 'How exciting! How lucky you are in Luggnagg, where a child has a chance of living for ever! And how especially lucky the Struldbrugs are! Disease, disaster, and death can never touch them! And imagine how much we can learn from them! I expect they're among the most important people in the country. They've lived through history and know so much, which they're certain to pass on to the rest of us. If I had the chance, I'd like to spend my whole life listening to the intelligent conversation of these extraordinary people, here in Luggnagg!'

'Well, of course,' answered my Luggnuggian friend with a smile, 'we'll be delighted if you stay longer with us. But I'd like to know how *you* would plan your life if *you* were a Struldbrug.'

'That's easy,' I replied. 'First I'd work hard, and earn a lot of money. In about two hundred years I'd be the richest man in Luggnagg. I'd study too, so that I knew more about everything than the cleverest professors. I'd also write down everything important that happened over the years, so that students of history would come to me for help. I'd teach young people what I had learnt. But most of my time

I'd spend with other Struldbrugs, friends of mine. Together we could help to destroy crime in the world, and begin to build a new and better life for everyone.'

I had only just finished describing the happiness of endless life, when I realized that my friend's shoulders were shaking and tears of laughter were running down his face.

'I really must explain,' he said. 'You see, you've made a very understandable mistake. You suppose that if someone lives for ever, he is young, healthy, and strong for ever too. And that doesn't happen. Our Struldbrugs have a terrible life. After living for about eighty years, they become ill and miserable. They have no friends and they can't remember much of the past. At that age the law considers them to be dead, so their children inherit their houses and money. Then they sometimes have to beg to get enough food to eat. They lose their teeth and hair, they forget the names of their families, and the only thing they want is to die. But that's impossible!'

I realized how stupid I had been, and felt very sorry for the poor Struldbrugs.

I finally left Luggnagg on a boat sailing to Japan. From there I found a ship which was returning to England. My voyage to Laputa, Balnibarbi, Glubbdubdrib and Luggnagg had taken me away from home for five and a half years.

12

A voyage to the country of the Houyhnhnms

It was not long before I started my next voyage, on 7th September, 1710, as captain of my own ship this time. The owner of the ship wanted me to sail to the Indian Ocean to do some business for him there, but I was very unlucky. On the way, I had to employ some new sailors from Barbados, but they were men of very bad character. I heard them whispering to the other sailors several times, but I did not suspect what they were planning. One morning, as we were sailing round the Cape of Good Hope, they attacked me and tied me up. They told me they were going to take

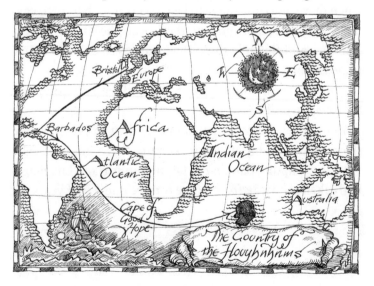

control of the ship and become pirates. There was nothing I could do. They left me, alone, on the beach of a small island in the middle of the Indian Ocean.

As the ship sailed away, I realized I had no idea where I was. I found a road away from the beach, and walked very quietly and carefully along, in case I was attacked. Several strange-looking animals were lying in a field, and some were sitting in a tree. Their heads and chests were covered in hair, and they had beards as well. They walked sometimes on two, and sometimes on four legs, and could climb trees. They were certainly the ugliest animals I had ever seen in all my travels.

When I met one of these creatures on the road, his face showed great surprise and he lifted a foot high in the air. I did not know if he was going to attack me or not, but I hit him hard with the side of my sword. He screamed so loudly that all the other animals ran to help him. There were about forty of them around me. I kept them away by waving my sword in the air, but their wild cries frightened me, and the horrible smell from their bodies made me feel sick.

Suddenly they all ran away. I noticed that a horse was coming along the road, so I supposed the animals were afraid of him. The horse stopped when he saw me, and seemed very surprised. He neighed several times in a very intelligent, gentle way, and I almost wondered if he was speaking in his own language. When another horse came along, the two horses walked up and down together, while neighing to each other. They seemed like two important people discussing a difficult problem. I watched this with astonishment, and decided that if the animals in this country seemed so sensible, the human beings must be the most intelligent in the world.

The two horses then came close to me, looking at my face and clothes with great interest. They talked to each other again, and then the first horse made clear signs for me to follow him.

He led me to a long, low building. Inside there were several large airy rooms, with no furniture. Other horses were sitting or lying comfortably on the floor, on clean blankets. But where was the master of the house? Were these horses his servants? I began to wonder if I was going mad. Then I realized that the house did not belong to a human, but to the horse who had brought me here. In this country, horses, not people, were in control.

I started learning a little of their language. Their word Houyhnhnm means a horse, and the word itself sounds very like the noise a horse makes. I found it very difficult to say this word, and so I decided to shorten it and call them Houys. Their servants were the horrible-looking animals I had seen earlier. They did all the hard work, and lived in dirty little rooms in another building, where they were tied to the walls. To my horror, these ugly animals, called Yahoos, had human faces which looked very similar to mine. I did not want anyone to think I was a Yahoo, so I tried to make it clear that my habits were very different from theirs. At least I was allowed to sleep in a separate room from them.

To my horror, these ugly animals, called Yahoos, had human faces which looked very similar to mine.

At first I thought I would die of hunger, as I could not eat the Yahoos' dirty meat or the Houys' grass and corn. But I soon learnt how to bake little cakes made of corn, which I ate with warm milk. Sometimes I caught a bird, and cooked it, or picked leaves of plants to eat with my bread.

My Houy master was very interested in me, and as soon as I could speak the language, he asked me to explain where I had come from.

'Well, master,' I neighed, 'I've come from a country on the other side of the world. And you may not believe this, but in my country all the important people look like Yahoos.'

'But how is that possible?' he asked gently. 'Your Houys surely wouldn't allow unintelligent creatures like Yahoos to control the country.'

'It may seem strange,' I agreed, 'but you see, *I* was surprised to find that in *this* country the Houys are the sensitive and intelligent creatures. And if I'm lucky enough to return home, I'll tell my friends all about it. But I'm afraid they may accuse me of lying.'

My master looked quite worried. 'What is lying?' he asked.

In their language there is no word which means telling lies, and my master had great difficulty in understanding me. I tried to explain.

'Oh,' he answered, still unsure. 'But why does anyone tell a lie? There's no reason for doing it. We use language in this country in order to understand each other, and to give and receive information. If you don't tell the truth, how *can* people understand each other?'

I began to see how different Houy life was from what I was used to.

'But tell me,' he continued, 'about your country.'

I was delighted to describe recent English history to him,

especially some of our most successful wars.

'But why does one country attack another?' he asked.

'There are many reasons,' I replied. 'A king or his lords may want more land. Or there may be a difference of opinion between two countries: for example, whether uniforms should be black, white, red or grey. Sometimes we fight because the enemy's too strong, sometimes because he isn't strong enough. Sometimes our neighbours want the things we have, or have the things we want, so we both fight until they take ours or give us theirs. We often attack our best friend, if we want some of his land. There's always a war somewhere. For this reason, being a soldier is one of the best jobs you can have.'

'A soldier,' repeated my master. 'I'm not quite sure what that is.'

'A soldier is a Yahoo who works for his King and country. His orders are to kill as many people as he can,' I answered.

'People who've never hurt him?' asked the Houy.

'That's right,' I said, pleased that he seemed to understand at last. 'Soldiers have killed thousands of people in recent history.'

He shook his head and looked sad. 'I think you must be – what was your word? Ah yes – *lying* to me. How could you and your countrymen kill so many other Yahoos? And why would you want to?'

I smiled as I replied proudly, 'Sir, you don't know much about European war. With our guns and bullets and gunpowder we can destroy a thousand ships, a hundred cities, and twenty thousand men. You see,—'

'Be quiet!' he ordered. 'I've heard enough. I know Yahoos are bad, but I didn't realize they could possibly do such terrible things.'

After these conversations I began to wonder whether the Houys were right. Why do we humans so often fight wars and tell lies? Peace and truth began to seem more important than making war or making money. I became more and more used to the Houys' ideas and way of life. As the Houys did, I hated the Yahoos for their dirty habits and unpleasant character. By the time I had been there a year, I walked and neighed like the Houys. I felt such a strong love for them that I planned to spend the rest of my life among them, and to try to become more like them. It is a great sadness to me, even today, that this was not possible.

One day my Houy master said, 'Can you explain something to me? Why are the Yahoos so violently fond of those shining stones in the fields? They dig for days to get them out of the ground, and hide them jealously from other Yahoos.'

'I expect they've found pieces of gold or silver,' I said. Because he did not seem to understand, I added, 'We use them as money, to pay for things, you see.'

'How strange!' he replied. 'We share everything here. No Houy needs – what do you call it? – *money*.'

Perhaps you can imagine how I felt. I knew I could be happy for ever with these sensible, gentle creatures, who never lied or stole, in a country which had no disease, no crime, no wars. But this perfect happiness did not last long.

'I'm sorry,' said my master one day. 'My friends and I

I knew I could be happy for ever with these sensible, gentle creatures.

have decided you can't stay here any longer. You see, you're neither one of us, nor a Yahoo.'

'No!' I cried desperately. 'Don't send me away! How can I go back to England to live with those awful Yahoos!'

'I'm afraid you must,' he replied gently. 'My servants will help you make a boat.'

And so, two months later, although I was very sad to leave, I said goodbye to my dear master and his family, and rowed away from the land of the Houys. I knew that I would never find happiness anywhere else.

I rowed away from the land of the Houys.

After several days travelling eastwards, I arrived in Australia, and from there managed to find a ship returning to Europe. I did not enjoy the voyage. The sailors all laughed at me because I walked and neighed like a horse. They looked just like those horrible Yahoos, and at first I could not let them touch me or come near me. Their ugly faces and unpleasant smell made me feel quite ill.

And when I arrived home in England, after being away for five years, my wife and children were delighted to see me, because they had thought I was dead. But to my horror they looked and smelt like Yahoos too, and I told them to keep away from me.

Even now, five years later, I do not let my children get close to me, although I sometimes allow my wife to sit with me while I eat. I try to accept my countrymen now, but the proud ones, who are so full of their own self-importance – well, they had better not come near me. How sad that people cannot learn from the Houys! I was hoping that perhaps human beings would change their ways after reading the stories of my life with the Houys. But they accuse me of lying in my book. And now I realize that people still lie, steal, and fight, just as they have always done, and probably will always do.

I will say no more. Clearly, there is no hope for human beings. I was stupid to think that I could bring reason and truth into their lives and thoughts. Humans are all Yahoos, and Yahoos they will remain.

GLOSSARY

astonishment   great surprise

attack *(v)*   to start fighting or hurting someone

crawl *(v)*   to move slowly on your hands and knees

creature   a living animal or person

entertainment   a show that people watch and enjoy

history   the study of the past

huge   very big

magician   someone who can make wonderful, strange things
  happen

magnet   a piece of iron that can pull other pieces of metal to it

master   a man who owns an animal, or who pays someone to
  work for him

mathematics   the study of numbers and shapes

neigh *(v)*   to make the noise that a horse makes

political   of government

professor   an experienced, older teacher who knows a lot

put out (**a fire**)   to make a fire stop burning

reward *(v)*   to give money or a present to someone to thank
  them for something

servant   someone who works (for example, cooking or cleaning)
  in another person's house

struggle *(v)*   to fight or to try to do something difficult

system (**of government**)   a way of doing things

tiny   very small

war   fighting between countries

Gulliver's Travels

ACTIVITIES

Before Reading

1 **Read the story introduction on the first page of the book, and the back cover. What do you know now about Gulliver and his travels? Choose words to complete this passage (one word for each gap).**

Gulliver visits some very _____ places. In a country called
Lilliput the human beings are much _____ than he is, and in
another country they are much, much _____. He meets _____
from the past, visits a _____ island and goes to a land where
_____ can talk. And during his travels he begins to _____ his
opinions about human beings and the _____ they live.

2 **How do you think Gulliver will be changed by his travels? Choose Y (yes) or N (no) for each of these ideas.**

When Gulliver finally returns to England, . . .

1 he will still think England is the best country in the world.
Y/N
2 he will still be proud of being human. Y/N
3 he will hate human beings and their ideas. Y/N
4 many of his own opinions will be different. Y/N
5 he will wish he could go back and live for ever in one of
the countries he has visited. Y/N
6 he will live happily with his family and his friends. Y/N
7 he will try to persuade people at home to live in a different
way. Y/N

ACTIVITIES

While Reading

Read Chapters 1 to 3. Choose the best question-word for these questions, and then answer them.

How / What

1 . . . did Gulliver arrive in Lilliput?
2 . . . was Gulliver's first experience of the Lilliputians?
3 . . . did the Lilliputians take Gulliver to their capital?
4 . . . did the King's officers find in Gulliver's pockets?
5 . . . did the King choose his officials?
6 . . . was the strange black thing found on the beach?
7 . . . was the difference between the Big-Endians and the Small-Endians?
8 . . . did Gulliver help Lilliput in the war with Blefuscu?
9 . . . did Gulliver protect his eyes from the Blefuscans' arrows?
10 . . . did the King want Gulliver to do next?
11 . . . did Gulliver put out the fire in the palace?

Before you read Chapter 4 (*Gulliver escapes from Lilliput*), can you guess the answers to these questions?

1 What punishment does the King decide on for Gulliver?
2 Do any of Gulliver's friends warn him of the danger?
3 Does Gulliver kill any Lilliputians during his escape?
4 How does he escape, and which country does he go to?
5 Where does he go next, and what does he take with him?

Read Chapters 5 and 6. Are these sentences true (T) or false (F)? Rewrite the false sentences with the correct information.

1 The sailors landed on Brobdingnag to look for gold.
2 Gulliver hid in the corn when the giants appeared.
3 The giants were about forty metres tall.
4 The farmer soon realized that Gulliver was an insect.
5 In the farmer's home Gulliver was attacked by rats.
6 Glumdalclitch took very good care of Gulliver.
7 The farmer took Gulliver all over the country to show him the sights.

Read Chapters 7 and 8, and answer these questions.

1 Why was the farmer glad to sell Gulliver to the Queen?
2 What did the King think Gulliver was at first?
3 What did the Queen's dwarf do to Gulliver?
4 Why was it unusual for foreigners to visit Brobdingnag?
5 Why was Gulliver able to go rowing or sailing?
6 What was the greatest danger to Gulliver in Brobdingnag?
7 What did the King want Gulliver to tell him about?
8 Why did the King refuse Gulliver's offer of gunpowder?

Before you read Chapter 9 (*Gulliver escapes from Brobdingnag*), what do you think is going to happen? Circle Y (yes) or N (no) for each of these ideas.

1 Glumdalclitch helps Gulliver to escape. Y/N
2 Gulliver uses gunpowder in order to escape. Y/N
3 A huge bird or an animal takes Gulliver away. Y/N

Read Chapters 10 and 11. Who said this, and who or what were they talking about?

1 'Go and see what you can buy and sell in the islands round here.'
2 'The earth was very nearly destroyed by the last one!'
3 'That's not much to look forward to, is it?'
4 'It's made us feel rather sick.'
5 'You'll find it a very interesting place.'
6 'You could ask them questions about their lives.'
7 'I drank too much and died of a fever.'
8 'In death, as in life, he has always been my friend.'
9 'I expect they're among the most important people in the country.'
10 'You see, you've made a very understandable mistake.'

Read Chapter 12, and answer these questions.

1 Why did Gulliver's sailors attack him and leave him on a small island?
2 Who was in control of this island?
3 Who were the servants in the country of the Houys?
4 What did Gulliver eat on the island?
5 Why did Gulliver have to explain to his Houy master what 'lying' meant?
6 What did Gulliver's Houy master think about money?
7 Why was Gulliver so happy in the land of the Houys?
8 Why did the Houys ask Gulliver to leave their country?
9 How did Gulliver feel about his family when he got home?
10 What did Gulliver realize five years later?

After Reading

1 These people are thinking about Gulliver. Who are they? Choose from the names below (you won't need all of them). Where was Gulliver, and what was happening at the time?

Glumdalclitch / the King of Brobdingnag / the ship's captain / Gulliver's wife / Flimnap / the King of Lilliput / Reldresal

1 'Telling us to keep away from him! I never heard of such a thing! You'd think he'd *want* to see his family after all this time! I can't understand what's the matter with him.'

2 'Such horrible, cruel ideas! I can't believe what he tells me is true. Do they really rob, and murder, and destroy each other like that? It must be an awful country to live in!'

3 'I'm sure my wife's going to the Man-Mountain's house again today. That's the third time this week! She thinks I haven't noticed anything, but I know what's going on!'

4 'Oh, I'm sure he's going to fall! Oh, poor little Gulliver! Can't someone climb up and rescue him? Oh, he's going to die, I know it! Someone must help him!'

5 'Well, I've sailed all over the world and I've never seen people as small as the ones he talks about. He must be mad, or lying! But then where did he get those tiny animals from? Perhaps he *is* telling the truth, after all.'

2 Here is a conversation between two of the Houys, who are discussing Gulliver. The first Houy is Gulliver's master. Complete the second Houy's side of the conversation.

Houy 1: What shall we do about the Yahoo-like animal? You know, the one who calls himself Gulliver.

Houy 2: _____

Houy 1: Oh yes, he speaks it quite well. Sometimes he can't explain things clearly, but he's very interesting to listen to.

Houy 2: _____

Houy 1: In my house, in a separate room well away from the Yahoos. He refuses to eat or sleep with them, you see.

Houy 2: _____

Houy 1: Because his habits are very different from theirs, he says. He keeps telling me he isn't a Yahoo at all.

Houy 2: _____

Houy 1: I know he does, but looks aren't the most important thing, are they? I must say, he's more intelligent than most of *my* Yahoos. But that's the problem, isn't it?

Houy 2: _____

Houy 1: Well, he isn't really a Yahoo, but he isn't one of us, either. So what shall we do with him?

Houy 2: _____

Houy 1: Back to his own country, you mean? But it sounds a very unpleasant place!

Houy 2: _____

Houy 1: Yes, perhaps you're right. At least he'll be with his own people again. He'll certainly be miserable if he stays here, because he'll never really be accepted, will he?

3 Here is a newspaper report of Gulliver's first adventure. Put the parts of sentences in the right order, and use these linking words to make a paragraph of four sentences.

after / and / but / however / that / when / where / which

1 _____ he promised not to hurt them in any way.

2 _____ came home, bringing some tiny cows and sheep

3 _____ he was no longer welcome in the country.

4 Mr Gulliver has just returned from an exciting voyage,

5 _____ they gave him his freedom

6 to prove that his strange stories about Lilliput are true.

7 _____ took him to the island of Lilliput,

8 Later, _____, Mr Gulliver was warned by a friend

9 _____ the people, he says, are only fifteen centimetres tall.

10 _____ hearing this, Mr Gulliver escaped from the island

11 At first these tiny Lilliputians kept Mr Gulliver in chains,

4 Complete this next report with words from the story.

Mr Gulliver has once again returned from his _____. This time, he tells us, he was in Brobdingnag, a land of _____, where the people were twenty metres tall. He was _____ by rats which were as big as _____, and he almost _____ in a bowl of milk! The King and Queen became so _____ of him that he stayed with them at their _____. The greatest _____ to him came when a huge _____ picked him up and ran up on to the palace _____, at least three hundred metres above the _____! Luckily, he survived this and other _____ situations, and has _____ his wife he will never go to sea again.

5 Here are some headlines for the two newspaper reports. Which ones go best with each report?

ENGLISHMAN IN TINY CHAINS A LUCKY ESCAPE

MR GULLIVER'S GIANT STORY IT'S A SMALL WORLD!

TALL STORIES FROM ABROAD! A TRAVELLER RETURNS

6 Do you agree (A) or disagree (D) with these ideas from the story? Why, or why not?

1 'It is more important to have a good character than to be clever or intelligent.'
2 'Why does anyone tell a lie? There's no reason for doing it.'
3 'Every problem can be solved by honest, sensible people.'
4 'Criminals must be punished, but people of good character must be rewarded.'
5 'Why do you need an army at all? You would not be afraid of any other country, if you were peaceful people.'
6 'The political life of a country must have no secrets and must be open for all to see and understand.'
7 'Clearly, there is no hope for human beings.'
8 'Humans are all Yahoos, and Yahoos they will remain.'

7 Which people or creatures in the story would you most like to meet? Which would you least like to meet? Explain why.

- A Lilliputian
- A Brobdingnaggian
- A Laputan
- A Struldbrug
- A Houyhnhnm
- A Yahoo

ABOUT THE AUTHOR

Jonathan Swift was born in 1667 in Dublin, Ireland, and was educated there, although both his parents were English. When he was twenty-two, he moved to England to work as a secretary to Sir William Temple. This gave him the chance to meet important people in English society and government, and he became very involved in the political life of the times. He returned to Ireland to become a priest, but continued to spend a lot of time in England, visiting his many friends.

During his life Swift published a great number of works, most of which were attacks on political and religious ideas. His writing made him many enemies in the church and government, but made his readers laugh at well-known people, and look with a fresh eye at fashionable ideas and beliefs.

In 1713 Swift became Dean of St Patrick's Cathedral in Dublin, and most of his remaining years were spent in that city. He continued with his political writing, and also worked hard to make life better for the Irish. He gave away a third of the money he earned to the poor, and spent another third on starting a new hospital, St Patrick's. His death in 1745 greatly saddened the Irish people.

Swift's most famous book, *Gulliver's Travels*, was published in 1726. It was a great success at the time and was read by everyone, from politicians to children. It is still enjoyed by readers of all ages today, both for its sharp attack on eighteenth-century ideas and customs, and for the amusing and fantastic adventures of its hero.

ABOUT BOOKWORMS

OXFORD BOOKWORMS LIBRARY

Classics • True Stories • Fantasy & Horror • Human Interest
Crime & Mystery • Thriller & Adventure

The OXFORD BOOKWORMS LIBRARY offers a wide range of original and adapted stories, both classic and modern, which take learners from elementary to advanced level through six carefully graded language stages:

Stage 1 (400 headwords)	Stage 4 (1400 headwords)
Stage 2 (700 headwords)	Stage 5 (1800 headwords)
Stage 3 (1000 headwords)	Stage 6 (2500 headwords)

More than fifty titles are also available on cassette, and there are many titles at Stages 1 to 4 which are specially recommended for younger learners. In addition to the introductions and activities in each Bookworm, resource material includes photocopiable test worksheets and Teacher's Handbooks, which contain advice on running a class library and using cassettes, and the answers for the activities in the books.

Several other series are linked to the OXFORD BOOKWORMS LIBRARY. They range from highly illustrated readers for young learners, to playscripts, non-fiction readers, and unsimplified texts for advanced learners.

Oxford Bookworms Starters   *Oxford Bookworms Factfiles*
Oxford Bookworms Playscripts   *Oxford Bookworms Collection*

Details of these series and a full list of all titles in the OXFORD BOOKWORMS LIBRARY can be found in the *Oxford English* catalogues. A selection of titles from the OXFORD BOOKWORMS LIBRARY can be found on the next pages.

Black Beauty

ANNA SEWELL

Retold by John Escott

When Black Beauty is trained to carry a rider on his back, or to pull a carriage behind him, he finds it hard at first. But he is lucky – his first home is a good one, where his owners are kind people, who would never be cruel to a horse.

But in the nineteenth century many people *were* cruel to their horses, whipping them and beating them, and using them like machines until they dropped dead. Black Beauty soon finds this out, and as he describes his life, he has many terrible stories to tell.

The Silver Sword

IAN SERRAILLIER

Retold by John Escott

Jan opened his wooden box and took out the silver sword. 'This will bring me luck,' he said to Mr Balicki. 'And it will bring you luck because you gave it to me.'

The silver sword is only a paper knife, but it gives Jan and his friends hope. Hungry, cold, and afraid, the four children try to stay alive among the ruins of bombed cities in war-torn Europe. Soon they will begin the long and dangerous journey south, from Poland to Switzerland, where they hope to find their parents again.

BOOKWORMS • THRILLER & ADVENTURE • STAGE 4

Treasure Island

ROBERT LOUIS STEVENSON

Retold by John Escott

'Suddenly, there was a high voice screaming in the darkness: "Pieces of eight! Pieces of eight! Pieces of eight!" It was Long John Silver's parrot, Captain Flint! I turned to run . . .'

But young Jim Hawkins does not escape from the pirates this time. Will he and his friends find the treasure before the pirates do? Will they escape from the island, and sail back to England with a ship full of gold?

BOOKWORMS • FANTASY & HORROR • STAGE 4

The Songs of Distant Earth and Other Stories

ARTHUR C. CLARKE

Retold by Jennifer Bassett

'High above them, Lora and Clyde heard a sound their world had not heard for centuries – the thin scream of a starship coming in from outer space, leaving a long white tail like smoke across the clear blue sky. They looked at each other in wonder. After three hundred years of silence, Earth had reached out once more to touch Thalassa . . .'

And with the starship comes knowledge, and love, and pain.

In these five science-fiction stories Arthur C. Clarke takes us travelling through the universe into the unknown but always possible future.

Desert, Mountain, Sea

SUE LEATHER

Three different parts of the world, but all of them dangerous, lonely places. Three different women, but all of them determined to go – and to come back alive!

Robyn Davidson walked nearly 3,000 kilometres across the Australian desert – with a dog and four camels.

Arlene Blum led a team of ten women to the top of Annapurna – one of the highest mountains in the world. Only eight came down again.

Naomi James sailed around the world alone, on a journey lasting more than 250 days.

Three real adventures – three really adventurous women.

I, Robot

ISAAC ASIMOV

Retold by Rowena Akinyemi

A human being is a soft, weak creature. It needs constant supplies of air, water, and food; it has to spend a third of its life asleep, and it can't work if the temperature is too hot or too cold.

But a robot is made of strong metal. It uses electrical energy directly, never sleeps, and can work in any temperature. It is stronger, more efficient – and sometimes more human than human beings.

Isaac Asimov was one of the greatest science-fiction writers, and these short stories give us an unforgettable and terrifying vision of the future.